DENIS WRIGLEY

The living world of the

WOODLAND

A Wrigley Eye Opener

LUTTERWORTH PRESS
Guildford and London

Isn't it quiet in the wood?
Here beneath the trees,
isn't it quiet?
Listen to the silence!
But when you listen carefully
you can hear lots of things.
The wood isn't a silent place.
It is full of tiny sounds...
rustling, humming, creaking, pattering sounds.

And your sounds, too, as you walk
on dried leaves... or tread on a twig!

Listen to the rustling of the wind-blown leaves.
Listen to the humming and buzzing of insects,
to the creaking of moving branches
and to the sudden movements of small animals...
and the flutter of birds.

The wood is alive
with living sounds: the building,
digging, eating, hunting, croaking, squeaking,
grunting sounds of living things.
There's a lot happening in the wood;
you can hear it and you can see it
if you look for it!

As you walk into this world of trees
and stand to listen,
the many and varied creatures
which inhabit the wood
will be looking at you
and listening to you,
ready to react to danger
or the threat to life that you might represent.
By being on the alert
life is preserved.

Often unseen but usually heard
are the birds of the wood.
Listen and you will hear
that each species has a different
song, recognised by its young
and others of its kind.
If you can learn
to recognise the sounds
you'll know which birds are living
in *your* woodland.

Just as sounds reveal hidden life
there are signs to look for, too.
Birds and animals leave tracks.
They also leave clues where they have been eating —
the shells of nuts,
the marks on trees and the damage
to young saplings.

   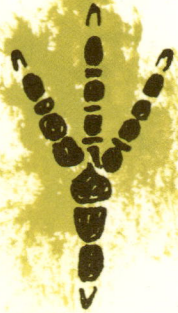

cloven hoof   paw mark

bird track

a nut showing the marks of nibbling

The wood which shelters this life
is a collection of trees.
Woods are only found where trees can grow —
where the soil and climate are good for growth.
The same kind of woodland is found
on low ground in cool countries
and high ground in hot countries.
Touch a tree trunk and feel the bark —
is it rough or is it smooth?
Look above you
at the branches bending to the breeze,
branches with twigs and twigs
with leaves.

It is the leaves which catch the sunshine,
and help to make the food
that the tree needs;
leaves of different sizes
and different kinds of leaves for different kinds of tree.
Pines and firs and elms and oaks, beeches
and ash trees, and many others;
each tree, each leaf different
and each leaf helping in the
life-making processes of the tree.

Leaf cells contain a substance
called chlorophyl.
Sunlight, working through the
chlorophyl, splits the water
in the leaf into hydrogen and oxygen.
The leaf breathes in carbon dioxide
from the air and the hydrogen
is added until a simple kind
of sugar is formed.
This is the food of the plant.

Some woods are composed of different kinds
of trees; others are made up of trees
of the same kind.
This is because some have grown naturally
whilst others have been planted as a crop
for their wood.
There are two types of tree:
deciduous, which lose their leaves
in autumn to grow new ones in spring,
and *coniferous*, which are often
called evergreens and usually
keep their cloak of green.

Trees use a lot of water;
so woodland only grows
where there is sufficient rainfall.
The tree roots spread wide and deep
and soak up the moisture
from the soil.
From the roots, it rises
up the tree in the sapwood and
carries with it minerals
and nitrogen.
Some of the sugar made in the leaf cells
is used to give energy for growth
and to build the cells and wood of the tree.
It travels to all parts in a fluid
called sap found in the
inner bark.

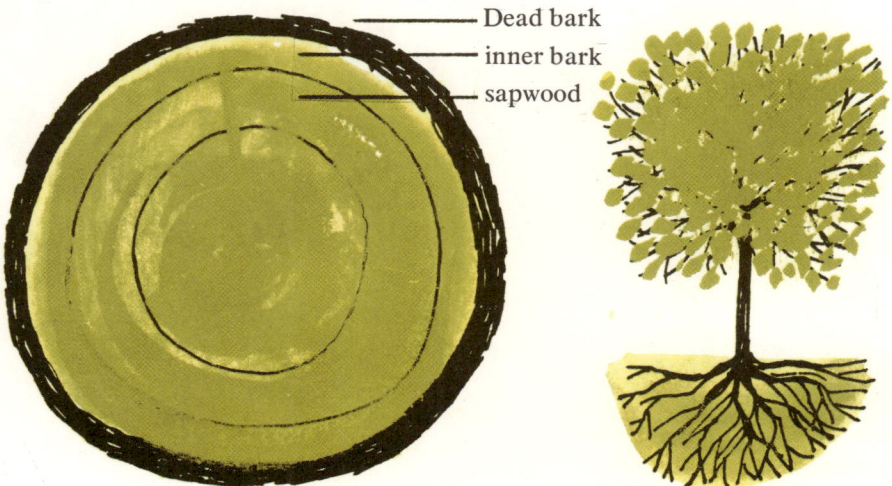

Dead bark
inner bark
sapwood

Look up to the roof of leaves
high amongst the branches of the trees.
Look at the birds of the woods,
fluttering and chattering and singing.
Swooping and gliding in flight,
they are at work above you as they carry
the materials to build nests
or insects or fruit or nuts as food;
different birds, large or small,
which depend on the wood for life.

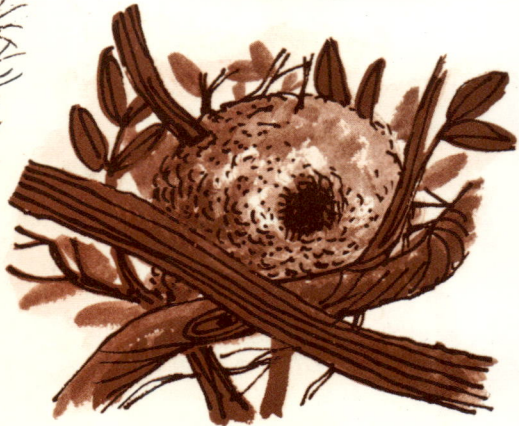

Often hidden behind leaves,
some nests are grouped together.
Some are alone.
Others provide protection
by having only a tiny entrance.

They are carrying insects and nuts and fruit
for these are a part of the woodland, too,
a part of the living woodland.
Some insects live in the bark of the
tree trunk; their young larvae
eat a pattern of passages in the bark.
Look closely.
(Did you touch that trunk?
Was it rough?
Or was it smooth?)

Other insects live in holes in trees,
or in rotting wood, in the ground
or on leaves.
Hidden from our sight and that of the birds
that would eat them, they use the cover of leaves
and stones and bark.
Their colours and patterns help them
to blend with the surface on which they live.
This natural protection from enemies
is so effective that you can look very closely
and still miss seeing them. We call this camouflage.

Insects such as bees
fly from flower to flower
in their search for nectar and pollen.
The pollen carried by the bees
helps to fertilise the flowers
and produce seeds.

When seeds are ripe they fall to the ground.
Some will be blown by the breeze
away from the tree they came from,
whilst others, held inside fruit,
will be taken by animals or birds,
or lie to sink into the ground as the fruit rots.
They will lie in the cold ground of winter till
the warmer days of springtime
before coming to life
and growing upwards into stems or trunks,
into twigs and leaves and flowers
to produce seeds once again...

Different methods of seed release:
The winged seed that is carried on the wind;
The cone that releases the seeds as it dries and opens;
The nut that contains the seed inside a cover which
splits open or rots to let the seed free.

For this is one of the ways in which plants
make new plants.
Each seed produces the same kind of plant
as the one from which it came.
So a violet seed can only make
another violet,
or the seed from a pine cone
can only produce a pine tree.

And as we stand in the wood
a new wood is growing around us
from seeds...
a new wood to take the place of the
old wood.
As old plants die — or are cut down —
new plants grow up
and the wood remains alive.

Here in this living wood
amongst the growing plants and trees
live other things, including
animals, birds and insects.
They exist because the wood exists, they
depend upon it and upon each other.
Animals and birds shelter in
the leaves and undergrowth and
feed from the fruits
and berries.
Animals and birds feed off the insects
of the woodland and off
other smaller animals.

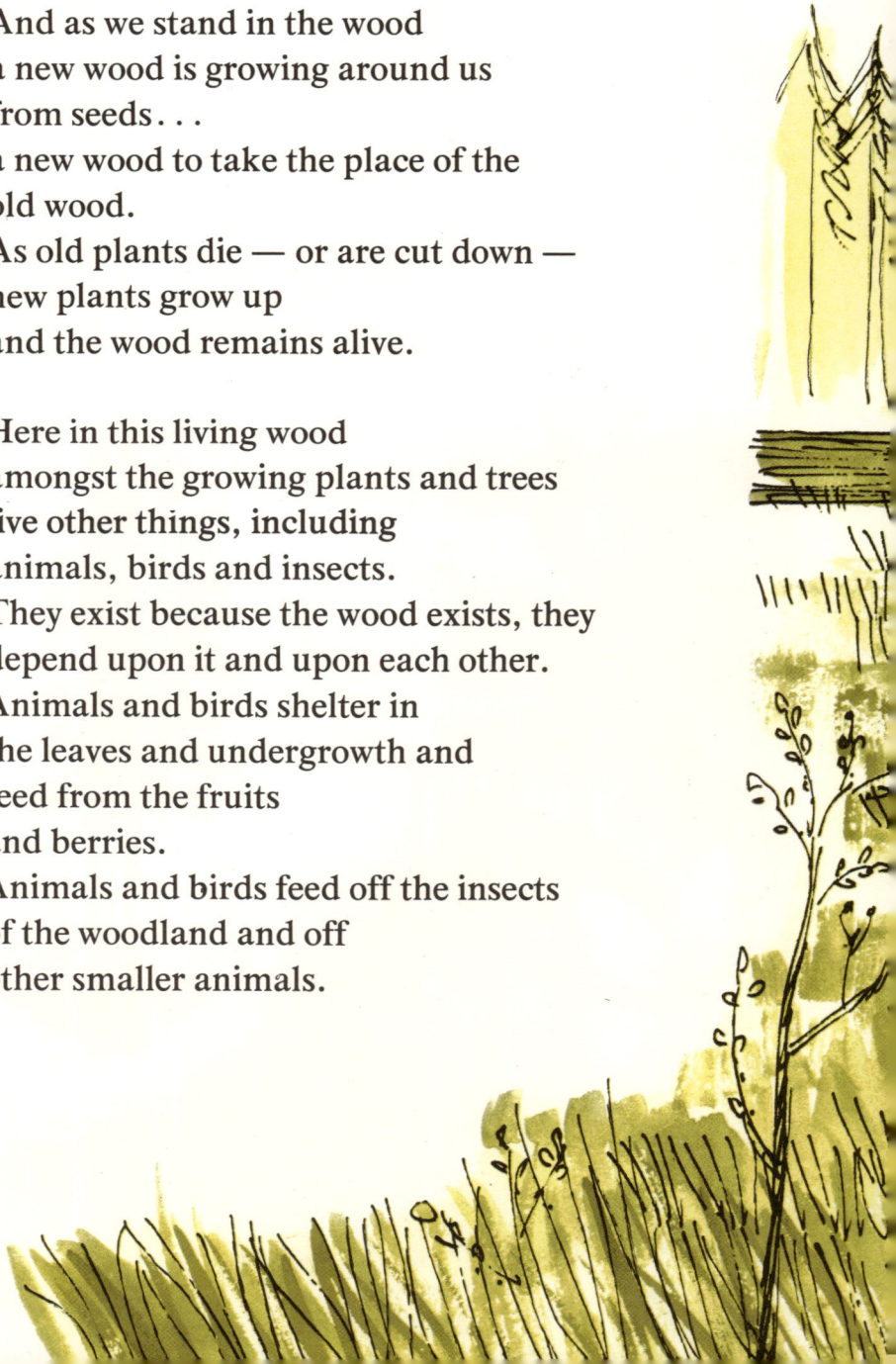

The air they breath is refreshed with oxygen
by the plant life. The plants provide
the food and shade and protection,
and the soil provides the nourishment
and holds the moisture that the plants need
for growth.
This is a world in which everything has a part to play.
If some of the woodland is damaged
by disaster or by the cutting saws of foresters,
the balance is destroyed
and the life that depends upon it dies
or moves to new ground.

Day and night the pattern of life
in the wood continues.
Sounds and movements
tell of the hunting,
searching activity.
In the daytime, animals hide
and animals feed — ready to run
or disappear if danger comes —
but safe from the world outside
the sheltering wood.

When night comes to the wood,
and many things are sleeping,
out come the night animals.
The night birds,
silently swooping
in search of unwary prey...
and the insects of night-time;
all are hunting for food
and that means that some
are hunting...
each other!

The litter of the woodland
lies on the surface of the ground.
Fallen leaves, branches
and the bodies of animals and birds
all decay and turn back
into the chemicals that will enter
the soil ready to supply
nourishment for new
and renewed life.

To help the processes of decay
grubs of beetles, insects and fungae
all live in or on the decaying matter.
They break it up and turn it gradually
into a rich *humus*.

Beneath this layer of rotting material
lies the *top* soil. This soil is
fertile and one in which plants can grow.
In this layer worms and insects live.
Further down below the top soil lies the *sub* soil
which has come from the wearing away
of the rocks beneath.
Here the only life is that
of burrowing animals and the occasional earthworm
seeking moisture in times of drought.

The roots of the trees stretch down
into the soil.
As well as providing the tree with water
from the soil, the roots are useful
to the tree in another way, too.
Without roots. . .
a tree would fall down!

In fact everything in the woodland
has a job to do.
Each living thing in the wood
is provided with the means
of maintaining life.
There are claws to scratch with,
teeth to bite, snouts to probe with,
tendrils to cling with and so on.
Look for yourself. It is
fascinating to find
the reason for everything.

See how the seasons
affect the life of the woodland.
Look in spring
when new life starts.

Look in summer
when the wood is full of leaf
and the new young life
is learning to live and move
here in the wood amongst the trees.

Look in autumn
when deciduous leaves
change colour and start to fall;
when some animals
store up food for the winter
and birds, visitors from another country,
fly away to return
when it is warmer again.

Look in winter
when bare branches
may reveal the nest that has been hidden
by leaves.
See how some animals
stand out clearly
and some blend
with the background.

When snow comes look for the
tell-tale tracks of birds and animals.
There's a lot to look for
and find out.
For example why is the conifer
shaped as it is?
And what would happen to a deciduous tree
if it kept its leaves
when there's a heavy snowfall?

Can you find out?
Can you?

First published 1977
Copyright © 1977 Denis Wrigley
ISBN 0 7188 2203 X
Printed in Hong Kong